THE PLAGUE

DIANE BAILEY

ROSEN
PUBLISHING®

New York

Published in 2011 by The Rosen Publishing Group, Inc.
29 East 21st Street, New York, NY 10010

Copyright © 2011 by The Rosen Publishing Group, Inc.

First Edition

Library of Congress Cataloging-in-Publication Data

Bailey, Diane, 1966–
The plague / Diane Bailey. — 1st ed.
    p. cm. — (Epidemics and society)
Includes bibliographical references and index.
ISBN 978-1-4358-9435-8 (lib. bdg.)
1. Plague—Juvenile literature. I. Title.
RC171.B295 2011
614.5'732—dc22

                                        2009046614

Manufactured in the United States of America

CPSIA Compliance Information: Batch #S10YA: For further information, contact Rosen Publishing, New York, New York, at
1-800-237-9932.

On the cover: The bacteria that causes the plague.

CONTENTS

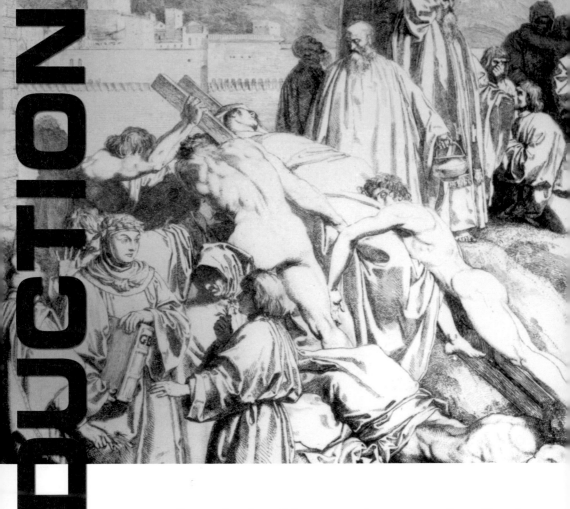

For a few horrible years, the streets of medieval Europe were filled with the sounds of death. People moaned in pain and wailed with grief. Church bells tolled for the dead. And carts rattled on the cobblestones as they carried away the bodies.

As plague gripped Europe in the middle of the fourteenth century, the normal business of living was replaced by the grisly spectacle of dying. Hundreds, then thousands, and eventually millions of people fell ill. People died in their homes and at their businesses. Sometimes they literally dropped dead in the streets.

Traditionally, when someone died, there was an elaborate ceremony. A priest led the mourners as

4

An engraving by Italian artist Luigi Sabatelli illustrates the nightmare of plague in Florence, Italy. Cities and villages collapsed into chaos as people died, filling the streets with corpses.

they carried the deceased person from his or her house to the cemetery. In the time of plague, this tradition collapsed. There were not enough caskets—the coffin makers could not keep up. There were not enough priests to hold the funerals. There were not enough places to bury the dead. Sometimes, there were not even enough people left to mourn.

Burials became nothing more than terrible chores. Men pushed carts through the streets and called out a grim order: "Bring out your dead." Families of those who had died in the night would then carry out the bodies and place them on the carts.

Collecting the dead was a horrible job that few wanted. Agnolo di Tura, an Italian man who lived during the plague, wrote, "No one could be found to bury the dead for money or for friendship." Many were afraid they would catch "the pestilence" from the bodies of the dead.

Anyone who would do the job was hired—including criminals. The *becchini* (gravediggers) in Florence, Italy, had a bad reputation. Florence was particularly hard-hit by the plague, but the becchini laughed in the face of death. While others mourned, they partied—and worse. They robbed and even murdered helpless people. There was no one to stop them. Sometimes they would burst into people's houses and demand money not to take people who were still alive.

The cemeteries filled up. New ones were built to keep up with the piles of bodies that grew each day. Even that was not enough. Soon, bodies were simply dumped into large "plague pits." However, Christians were concerned with getting a proper funeral that would guarantee they went to heaven. To fulfill this spiritual need, Pope Clement VI blessed the entire Rhone River, making it sacred. Bodies were then put into the river and floated out to the Mediterranean Sea.

The plague raged through the Mediterranean, into Italy, France, England, and northern Europe. Before it stopped, it killed twenty-five million people—about a third of the continent's population. Some modern historians think the number could have been as high as fifty million—60 percent of the population.

History is made by people. Usually, they make it by what they do in their lifetimes. But in the case of the plague, history was made by death. The horrible toll of the plague changed the face and fabric of Europe forever.

CHAPTER ONE

THE PESTILENCE

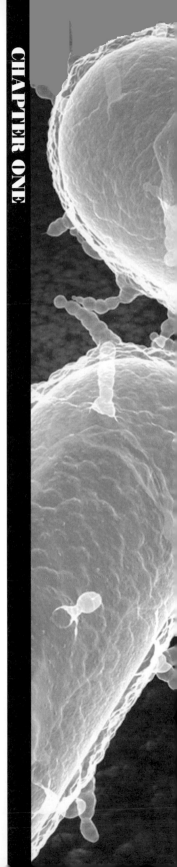

Rumors floated in from traders and sailors. A strange, terrible disease was moving through the Mediterranean. The people who got it suffered from extreme pain. Then, they passed the sickness to others. Worst of all, they died. The pestilence seemed to strike down nearly everyone it touched.

People who lived in Europe in the mid–1300s probably didn't know what to make of these stories. At first, they probably did not worry too much about a disease that killed far-away people. Perhaps they thought it would not affect them. They would be wrong. Within months of those first frightening reports, the pestilence was moving north—into the heart of Europe.

A Disease of Rodents

Plague did not start out as a human disease. It began in rodents. Marmots, a type of large squirrel in Asia, were probably the first to get it. Rats, prairie dogs, and other rodents got the disease, too.

The plague is caused by a bacterium called *Yersinia pestis*. It evolved out of an ancient

7

bacterium that caused stomach flu symptoms but was ultimately not fatal. However, the plague bacterium was ambitious. It evolved into an efficient killer.

These bacteria live in fleas, which in turn live on rodents. People don't feel much sympathy for sick fleas, but fleas infected with plague suffer, too. Fleas survive by feeding on their hosts (the animals they live on). They bite their hosts, taking in a small amount of blood each time. The plague bacteria interfere with this process. The bacteria block the flea's stomach so it never feels full. The hungry flea keeps eating. However, there is nowhere for the blood to go. The flea then spits the blood back into the wound made by its bite. Along with the blood comes a few plague bacteria. Now the flea's 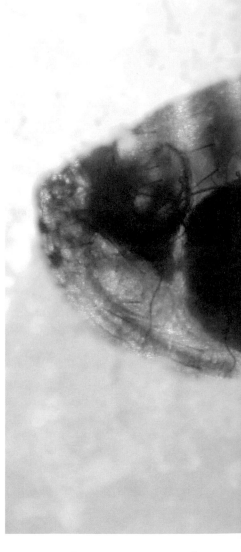 host animal is also infected. Plague is not always transmitted through "blocked" fleas. Some fleas can spread it just by having the bacteria on their mouths.

Making the Leap

In medieval Europe, people were surrounded by garbage. In cities, people lived extremely close together. The streets were

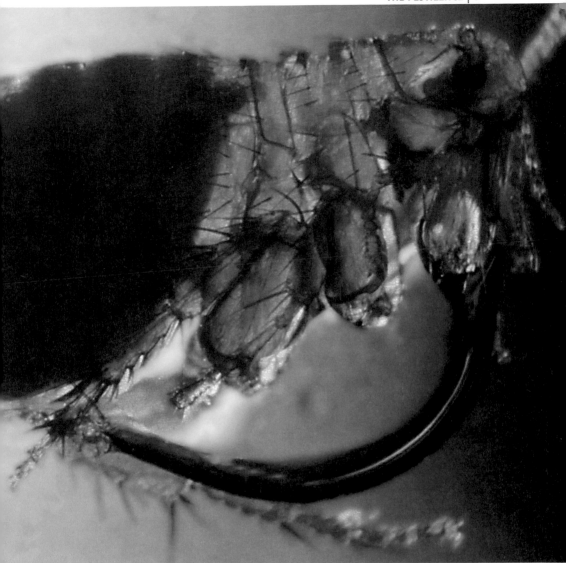

A magnified picture of a diseased flea shows its body filled with the blood it sucked from a mouse. The plague bacteria makes fleas spit infected blood back into their victims, spreading the disease.

filled with human and animal waste. People did not know how to effectively get rid of it. (In many cases, good sanitation only meant warning people on the street before dumping a bucket of slop out the window.) People were certainly aware of the "ick" factor. However, they did not fully understand that waste could actually be dangerous. The garbage attracted rats—and their fleas carried the plague.

It was a disgusting place, but not to rats. Rats liked what humans rejected. The amount of waste grew. So did the number of rats who were attracted to it. When these rats became infected with plague, it was only a matter of time before it spread to humans.

Rat fleas don't particularly like human blood. They much prefer rats. However, the rats were dying of plague. A dead body is no place to live—even for a flea. The fleas had to move. In medieval Europe, the closest vacancy was usually on a human.

Plague is not carried only by rat fleas. Some historians believe that in the fourteenth century, human fleas might have helped transmit the disease. Also, sometimes fleas don't need to be the messenger at all. Certain forms of plague are contagious between humans.

Three Types of Plague

The plague comes in three forms. The most common is the bubonic plague. Without treatment, bubonic plague kills about half of the people who get it. It usually takes several days to a week, although some people survive longer. Hanging on for a few extra days isn't necessarily a good thing, though. The plague is one of the most hideous and painful diseases known to humans.

Victims of plague start by getting flu-like symptoms, such as headaches, chills, and fever. But then the disease really takes hold. Patients develop a red rash. Then come stomach cramps. They vomit until there is nothing left and then continue to retch. They get black, tarry diarrhea. Their breath is short and blood pressure low. They become weak and

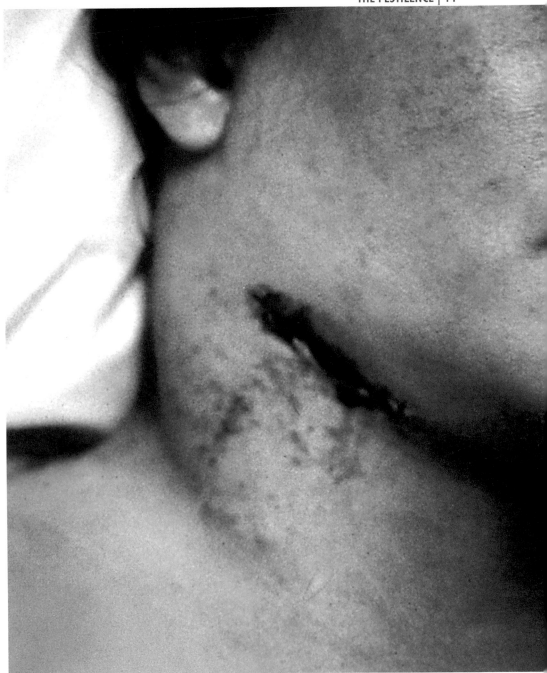

Bubonic plague gets its name from buboes, swollen areas under the skin caused by inflamed lymph nodes. An irritated bubo is shown on this plague victim's neck.

confused, and, not surprisingly, they have trouble sleeping. They thrash around violently.

Lymph nodes swell under the skin, forming buboes. (Bubonic plague takes its name from this word.) Buboes can grow to the size of an egg. They usually form in the groin, in the armpits, or on the neck. They are extremely painful. If the patient lives long enough, buboes can be punctured and drained. This aids in recovery.

Despite the gruesome progress of bubonic plague, if someone is going to get plague, bubonic is the best type. The other two are worse. In a case of pneumonic plague, the bacteria infect the lungs. Pneumonic plague is highly contagious. The bacteria live in the water droplets in the lungs so that whenever the victim coughs, sneezes, or even breathes, the plague bacteria move into the outside air. Whoever happens to be standing next to the plague victim may breathe in the infected air. Not only is pneumonic plague more contagious, it works faster and is more deadly. Without medicine, it kills almost 100 percent of its victims, usually within a couple of days. Even with modern treatment, pneumonic plague still can take half of its victims.

Septicemic plague is a rare third type of plague. Septicemic plague is an infection of the blood caused by the plague bacteria. Bleeding under the skin causes the skin to turn black. Patients usually die within a couple of days, and sometimes even faster.

Crazy Weather We're Having

In the 1340s, a few years before the plague began, Europe's weather forecasts were predictable: rain, rain, and more rain. The continent was soaked. This should have been good news for people who had trouble growing enough food. However, the

Ring Around the Rosy

A red rash, sneezing—and eventually death. The symptoms of the plague match the seemingly cheerful words of the children's rhyme "ring-around-the-rosy." It is commonly thought that this rhyme was invented after a plague epidemic in the 1600s in England. The first line describes the victims' skin rash, which is red or rosy in color. "A pocketful of posies" refers to the practice of carrying sweet-smelling items to ward off the disease. The line "ashes, ashes" might refer to the custom of burning dead bodies. Or, it could be that the words originally said "achoo, achoo," mimicking the sound of sneezing. The final line, "we all fall down," describes death.

However, these interpretations could be wrong. There is no known printed record of this song before 1881, when the Mother Goose rhymes were published. The first time an author suggested it was tied to the plague was in 1961. Many folk historians now believe the rhyme started as just a rhyme.

rain destroyed many of the crops while it increased the amount of wild plant growth. This meant there was more food for rodents. Their populations increased. Some moved into human areas. When plague broke out in rodent populations, it killed the rats and started seeking out other hosts.

Natural disasters have also been tied to outbreaks of the plague. Just prior to the outbreak of the plague in the fourteenth century, earthquakes and volcanic eruptions were reported. People thought the ash that billowed from volcanoes created miasmas. Miasmas are clouds of polluted air. People believed God sent them to punish mankind for its sin.

Although most modern scientists do not believe that natural disasters directly cause the plague, this theory had an aspect of truth to it. Disasters disrupt the normal flow of life. People

Men in San Francisco, California, caught and killed rats to help stop a plague epidemic that spread through the city in the early 1900s. Rat catching paid up to fifty cents per rat.

and animals may be forced out of their homes. Then they can come into contact with each other—and spread disease.

In 1906, a powerful earthquake rocked San Francisco, California. Rats were forced onto the streets—and an epidemic

of plague started. In 1994, a plague epidemic in India also followed an earthquake that had happened the year before.

Plague came to Vietnam in the 1960s. This outbreak may have been caused by a man-made disaster. Vietnam and the United States were at war. The U.S. Army dropped a poison called Agent Orange on the dense forests of Vietnam. It killed the trees. This may have disrupted the rodent populations, driving them out into closer contact with humans. Thousands of people died from the plague. Most plague epidemics live and die within animal populations. When they do spread to humans, the effects can be catastrophic.

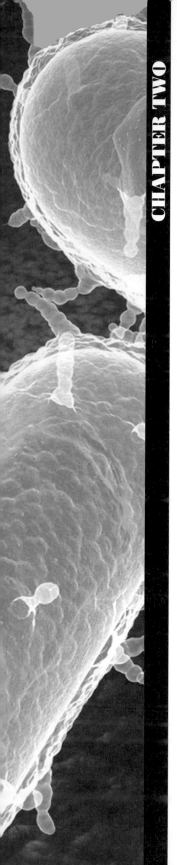

CHAPTER TWO

THE THREE PANDEMICS

Fast-acting and long-lasting! It sounds like an advertisement for cold medicine. Unfortunately, it's also an accurate description of plague. Plague is a bad guest. Not only does it usually kill its host, it won't leave.

A pandemic is when a disease spreads worldwide, affecting many people in many different areas. A plague pandemic can last hundreds of years. Throughout history, there have been three recorded plague pandemics.

The Plague of Justinian

In the early years of the sixth century, the Byzantine (Eastern Roman) Empire was ruled by the emperor Justinian. He lived in the empire's capital, Constantinople (now Istanbul, Turkey). Justinian had big political goals. He wanted to increase the size and influence of the Roman Empire.

For many years, Justinian was successful. He worked to conquer parts of Europe and Africa. However, his efforts came to an abrupt halt in 542 CE. Not even the powerful and wealthy Roman Empire could fight the plague.

The powerful Roman emperor Justinian is memorialized in a mosaic designed during his rule in the sixth century. An outbreak of plague stopped Justinian's efforts to enlarge the Roman Empire.

Historians aren't sure exactly how the plague entered Constantinople. It may have started in Africa and moved north through Egypt. People in Constantinople ate grain that came from Egypt. Justinian built a huge storehouse for this grain. It's likely rats would have been attracted to it. Silk and linen—which may have had fleas hiding in them—also came from Egypt. Another possibility is that traders brought infested goods from central Asia.

Justinian himself caught the plague, although he survived. However, his empire was crippled. Trade stopped. Food production stopped. Even the wars stopped. There simply weren't enough people left.

In the years that followed, farmland in Africa withered because the irrigation systems there were left untended. The Sahara desert pushed into areas that had been productive wheat fields.

The Name of Death

If you asked a person in 1350 what the Black Death was, he or she might have given you a funny look. Modern people refer to that plague epidemic as the Black Death. At the time, however, it was known as "the pestilence" or "the great mortality."

The name "Black Death" didn't come into common use until the eighteenth century. It was used then to describe the epidemic of the 1300s, as opposed to London's Great Plague of 1665. Many people assume the "black" refers to how victims' skin sometimes turned black from internal bleeding. However, the name is probably a misinterpretation of the Latin term *atra mors*. *Mors* means "death." *Atra* means "terrible" but can sometimes be translated as "black."

One result of this plague pandemic was that as the Byzantine Empire literally dried up, western Europe became more isolated. It evolved separately from the rest of the empire and developed its own cultures.

The Black Death of Europe

Most historians believe that the plague of the fourteenth century began in the Far East, perhaps China, or on the Asian steppes. The steppes are vast grasslands between China and the Caspian Sea. Traders then carried the plague into Europe. However, other historians believe that trade between Asia and Europe had slowed down in the years leading up to the plague, and that the disease came from somewhere closer to Europe.

Wherever it started, it's clear that by 1347 it reached Kaffa (now Feodosiya), a city on the Black Sea in an area of Europe called Crimea (now Ukraine). In that year, an army of Tatar warriors attacked an Italian settlement in Kaffa. However, the Tatars weakened as plague tore through their ranks. Soldier upon soldier fell. Desperate, the Tatars launched a new weapon: their own dead. They catapulted the bodies over the wall of the city of Kaffa, perhaps hoping to spread the plague to their enemies.

This is one of the first known instances of attempted "bioterrorism." Modern science tells us that the Tatars' approach probably wouldn't have worked—corpses aren't contagious. However, no wall or soldier could keep the fleas out. Within days, the townspeople of Kaffa had caught the disease. The Italians fled home, taking the plague with them. When they docked in Sicily, an island off the Italian mainland, the sailors were already dying. Fearful, the Sicilians ordered the sailors back onto their ships and sent them away. It was too late. Plague was already there.

The Tatars were infected with plague when they attacked Italian traders in what is now the Ukraine. Here they are shown a few decades later, battling Russian armies.

Meanwhile, trading ships were arriving at other ports in Italy and the rest of Europe. Silk, spices, and other exotic goods came first into Constantinople, carried by traders from the East. From there they continued west to Italy and then north into the rest of Europe. People welcomed the luxuries

the traders brought. However, nestled in a bolt of fabric or a sack of grain rode a tiny hitch-hiker: the flea. By the winter of 1348, plague had broken out all along the coastal cities of the Mediterranean Sea.

Plague continued north, into Spain, France, and England. It raged until about 1351. In these few years, Europe was transformed, just as the Byzantine Empire had been nine hundred years earlier. Entire families died. Smaller villages were completely wiped out.

No one knows exactly how many died. It was impossible to keep an accurate count. However, each person was keenly aware of how the plague touched him or her personally. Within a family, the math was easy. One Italian man wrote in his account, *The Plague in Siena*, "I, Agnolo di Tura … buried my five children with my own hands."

Was the Black Death Plague?

Some historians and scientists believe the Black Death was not the bubonic plague. They say it moved too far, too fast, and was too deadly. Suggestions have been made that the disease was actually something else. One scientist studied tree rings and believes comets hit the earth about that time. These could have produced chemical reactions in the air that caused widespread sickness—but not from plague.

It's true that bubonic plague is not very contagious, and fleas don't thrive in cold temperatures. However, the Black Death spread into the cold regions of northern Europe. If it were carried by rats, then why are there no accounts of dead rats lying around? And how did rats—which aren't big on traveling—spread all over Europe?

One possible explanation is that the disease was the pneumonic plague. This type of plague can survive colder temperatures and pass from person to person. Also, it might have been fleas—not rats—that were doing the traveling. Although fleas prefer living on warm bodies, they can survive for several months in animal burrows, stores of food, or clothing.

Another possibility is that the fourteenth-century plague was a strain capable of surviving better than the particularly strong form of the disease that we see today.

The Third Pandemic

In 1855, plague broke out in the Yunan province of China. It took about forty years for the plague to take hold this time, but eventually it spread throughout the country. In 1894, in the city of Canton, sixty thousand people died in just a few weeks. From there, it jumped to Hong Kong. That city suffered one hundred thousand deaths in two months.

By the mid-1800s, travel was much more sophisticated than it had been five hundred years earlier. Shipping was more widespread. Trains could carry people at speeds far faster than the horses of the Byzantine Empire or medieval Europe.

Le Petit Journal

ADMINISTRATION
61, RUE LAFAYETTE, 61
Les manuscrits ne sont pas rendus
On s'abonne sans frais
dans tous les bureaux de poste

5 CENT. SUPPLÉMENT ILLUSTRÉ 5 CENT.

22me Année — Numéro 1.057

DIMANCHE 19 FÉVRIER 1911

ABONNEMENTS

SIX MOIS | UN AN
SEINE et SEINE-ET-OISE.. 2 fr. | 3 fr. 50
DÉPARTEMENTS........... 2 fr. | 4 fr. »
ÉTRANGER.... .... 2 50 | 5 fr. »

LA PESTE EN MANDCHOURIE

A French publication illustrates the plague that broke out in Manchuria in the early twentieth century. Death (the "Grim Reaper") is represented by a skeleton carrying a scythe, which he uses to kill people.

Because of this, the third pandemic of plague was the first to truly go global. It reached Japan and India in 1896. By 1899, it had traveled thousands of miles south, to South Africa. That same year, it hit Hawaii. A year later, in 1900, it had reached San Francisco, California. Eventually, it infected people on every continent except Antarctica—which had no people.

The plague slowed down over the next fifty years, although major outbreaks still occurred. In Manchuria, about sixty thousand people died in 1910. Another sixty thousand died a decade later in 1920. During its first one hundred years, the third pandemic killed people everywhere it went, although most of them—about twelve million—were in China and India. The third pandemic, called modern plague, continues to this day with occasional outbreaks.

Aftermath

A plague pandemic is unpredictable. Sometimes it creeps slowly. Other times it spreads with frightening speed. On the backs of its victims, it can climb mountain ranges and cross oceans. It can give its deadly gift to anyone who crosses its path. And then—for seemingly no reason—it vanishes, hiding among animals until it is ready to come out again.

By the time the third pandemic began, the world's population had grown again after the Black Death and was larger than it had ever been. The disease spread across the entire world, but as a species, humans were able to withstand it. The way people lived had changed in the previous five hundred years. There was more communication and contact between people, which made them more vulnerable to the plague. But there were also improvements in sanitation and medical treatment. During the third pandemic, scientists got to know the enemy. They identified the plague bacteria and its source. They also developed ways to kill it. For these reasons, the disease did not destroy the bigger "way of life"—not as it did during the Black Death.

Several first-hand accounts survive from the Black Death, and even seven hundred years later, scientists can study physical evidence—such as graves and bones—to find out what happened. However, all history is incomplete. Looking back at the Black Death, it is almost certain that we've missed some details and gotten others wrong. But the picture we do have—of what happened during and after this catastrophe—shows how disease can change a society forever.

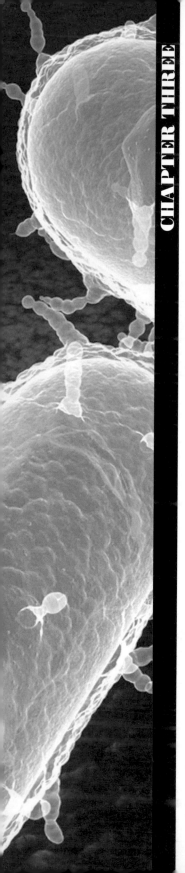

CHAPTER THREE

DESPERATE TIMES

In medieval Europe, no one escaped the horror of the plague. Families were ripped apart. Death took some. Survivors were terrified they would die—or felt guilty that they survived when others had not. Panic and despair took over. The old rules were not obeyed. New ones—or none at all—took their place.

Looking for a Cause

Nobody knew about germs in medieval times. But obviously something had to cause the plague. One school of thought said the disaster was because Saturn and Jupiter were lined up in a certain way. Another explanation blamed earthquakes in Europe and Asia for releasing deadly fumes.

Most theories came down to the same answer: God. Whatever method God had used, many thought he was unhappy with the sinful ways of people. Did he disapprove of the theater? The opera? Perhaps he didn't like those fashionable long-pointed shoes people were wearing.

People prayed for forgiveness. Most of all, they prayed for God to stop the plague. The Catholic Church was the backbone of society in Europe. People believed clergy members were a

In this engraving, a priest is surrounded by dying people as he kneels in the street and appeals to God to stop the plague. Many clergymen died from plague as they tended to people.

hotline to God. They turned to their priests for help. However, the church was as helpless as everyone else. People did not understand why God was so merciless.

At first, many people blamed their own sinful ways for the plague. As the crisis continued, they looked for other scapegoats. They found one in the Jews. Anti-Semitism—prejudice against Jewish people—did not start as a result of the plague. In fact, it had been going on for hundreds of years. The plague was only the most recent excuse to blame Jews.

Most people in medieval Europe were Christians. They tolerated Jews, but they did not always trust them. During the plague, this distrust got worse. Jews were allowed to do fewer and fewer things.

People were desperately looking for a way to explain the plague. It didn't matter how unreasonable this explanation was. Jews were accused of poisoning public water wells. (For religious reasons related to hygiene, many Jews did not use the city wells.) Some Christians said that Jews were killing Christians in an evil plot to control the world. Of course, these accusations were total nonsense. Under torture, however, Jews confessed to crimes they had not committed. They were punished by death. Pope Clement VI formally condemned the practice of killing Jewish prisoners, but it still continued.

From Quarantines to Cologne

Medieval medicines were useless against the plague—but that didn't stop people from trying. Dozens of herbal remedies appeared on the shelves of the apothecaries (drugstores). Desperate people were willing to try just about anything.

One common belief was that plague was caused by bad air. Burning certain herbs and plants was supposed to clean the air. Housewives set out dishes of milk to absorb poisonous

A page from a fifteenth-century medical book, *Tractatus de Pastilencia*, shows a person tending to the infected bodies of plague victims.

air. City officials rang bells and fired guns in order to move the air around. Supposedly, moving air would let the poison escape and float away. People also splashed on cologne or carried sweet-smelling pouches. One observer noted that people who worked among public toilets became ill less often. People wondered if the smell made them stronger. Bending over a latrine was nauseating, but it was better than dying. People tried it.

Physicians advised patients to eat light meals and limit their physical activity. However, basic hygiene was ignored. Washing would have helped to kill germs and get rid of fleas. But staying clean was not considered important, since people did not yet understand the connection between staying clean and being "germ-free."

To some extent, people did recognize a link between disease and poor sanitation. However, they did not understand it. People did not know germs caused disease. They thought that odors were to blame. In 1349, England's King Edward III ordered the mayor of London to clean the city's streets. Laws were passed to limit the work of butchers and tanners, since they worked with dead, smelly animals. Unfortunately, the problem was far more serious than unpleasant smells.

The best defense against plague was to not catch it in the first place. People quarantined the sick until they got better (or died). Sometimes they went to the extreme. They locked people inside their homes, with no way out, until they died from either disease or starvation. Quarantines were a good idea in theory, but they didn't work very well in practice. Compassionate citizens still took care of the sick and sometimes got sick themselves. Also, although the quarantines could fence in people, they could not contain the fleas.

As people continued to die, doctors were feared and mistrusted. They were criticized for charging money for their

Plague doctors wore masks with beaks filled with herbs to protect them from the smell of death. The frightening costume of the "beak doctor" told people that plague was near.

services when they could not help. Even their appearance was frightening. To protect themselves from the disease, doctors wore long robes with hoods. Attached to the hood was a mask with a beak that held herbs to cover the stench of death. These outfits became a terrifying symbol of the plague.

Fight or Flight

The natural response to the plague was fear. This changed to flat-out terror when people realized they were absolutely helpless. An ancient human instinct set in. When threatened, humans do one of two things: fight or take flight. Fighting was pointless, so many tried flight.

Fear was stronger even than family ties. Healthy people left the sick to fend for themselves. Husbands deserted their wives. Parents abandoned their children. An Italian man, Marchione di Coppo Stefani, wrote in *The Florentine Chronicle* that "Many died with no one looking after them…When someone took to bed sick, another in the house, terrified, said to him: 'I'm going for the doctor.' Calmly walking out the door, the other left and did not return again."

Those who remained struggled to care for each other. In medieval times, everyone helped keep a family running. Adults worked at a trade or in a family business to bring in income. Children were expected to contribute as well.

Plague victims, identified by the red rash on their faces, receive a blessing in this illuminated manuscript from the fourteenth century.

Death meant that there were fewer people to do the work. As time went on, however, there was less work to do. Society was falling apart. Merchants and craftsmen had no customers. Laborers had no jobs.

Nobles and wealthy merchants fled the cities, hoping to protect themselves in the country. Some clergy members also left. However, many of them found the courage and compassion to remain with the sick.

The people running from the towns did not know that in many cases, the race was already over. They were taking the plague with them. Fleas already lived on their bodies or nested in their clothes and belongings. People died during their travels, collapsing at the side of the road. Those that had the strength continued on—until the plague took them as well.

Slipping Standards

The plague gripped Europe tighter and tighter. Habits and rituals that regulated people's everyday lives began to disintegrate.

Businesses closed down. Cathedrals stayed half-built. Government officials stopped doing their jobs. In 1348, the Hundred Years War (1337–1453) between England and France was temporarily stopped because so many soldiers died. Farmers who sold food stayed out of the cities. This made food harder to find. It was more expensive when it was available.

People cowered in their homes, afraid to go out and expose themselves to illness. Some people hid their sick family members, afraid that their friends and neighbors would turn against them. Homes with sick people were marked with a special flag. People—even doctors—often refused to enter a house known to have plague. Proper funerals were abandoned. The dead were tossed into trenches or left to pile up in the streets.

The Flagellants

If sin was the cause of the plague, then to repent was the answer. That was what men in the Brotherhood of the Flagellants believed. They thought the plague was God's way of showing his displeasure. If they showed they were sorry by punishing themselves, maybe God would ease the plague. With metal-tipped leather whips, they whipped (flagellated) their naked backs three times a day for approximately thirty-three days—one day for each year of Christ's life. They gave up nearly every creature comfort. They did not bathe, sleep in beds, change their clothes, or even talk to each other without permission.

They marched into the towns of Europe to put on their grisly show. Townspeople gathered to watch, hoping that the actions of the flagellants would save them, as well. The church tolerated the flagellants at first, but their gatherings became more and more disruptive. Eventually Pope Clement VI spoke out against them, saying their actions did not support the beliefs of the church.

A group of flagellants march into a Belgian city during the plague. Flagellants often wore distinctive clothes, such as these white robes.

The church was in an enormously difficult position. Clergy members died the same as everyone else. God hadn't given them any special protection from the plague. Also, the number of deaths meant there was a greater demand for priests. They had two jobs: tend to the dying and comfort the living.

The church made radical changes. Confession is a Catholic ritual where a person admits his or her sins to a priest. There were not enough priests to hear confessions. The church decided that anyone—even women—could hear confessions. Last rites are another important part of the Catholic religion. Someone about to die is given a final blessing. People were dying too fast for everyone to get last rites, however. The church ruled that when it was impossible to receive last rites, they could simply be skipped.

Because there was a desperate need for priests, the church lowered the minimum age necessary to become one. However, these new priests were inexperienced. They were often less committed.

Some people turned to religion in the time of the plague. Going to church and praying brought them comfort. But other people felt that God had given up on them. They stopped going to church. Some also stayed away because they did not want to come into contact with sick people.

Dying people wrote hasty wills. Sometimes they gave everything to the church in a last attempt at salvation. This left children and other family members with nothing—except the hope that things would get better.

As the plague finally came to an end, families and towns had been beaten, battered, and ripped apart. The process of healing seemed overwhelming, but slowly it happened. Shock and despair faded. The business of living took over once again. It was not easy, but it was life.

Myths and Facts

MYTH If you catch the plague, you will die.

FACT Though the plague killed around twenty-five million people during the Black Death, the discovery of the bacterium that causes it combined with prompt care and antibiotics makes it likely that someone who contracts the plague today will survive.

MYTH All rats are filthy disease-ridden animals.

FACT Despite their reputation, many types of rats are very useful, intelligent creatures. Some species of rats are used for research in psychology, medicine, and other fields. Many people also keep domestic rats as pets.

MYTH The Great Fire of London stopped the plague in 1666.

FACT While the fire may have slowed the progression of the plague by wiping out rats, some experts believe that improvements in the diet of people during that time or possibly a mutation in the plague bacteria was more likely the cause of the plague's waning. But the disappearance of the plague during this time remains a mystery to this day.

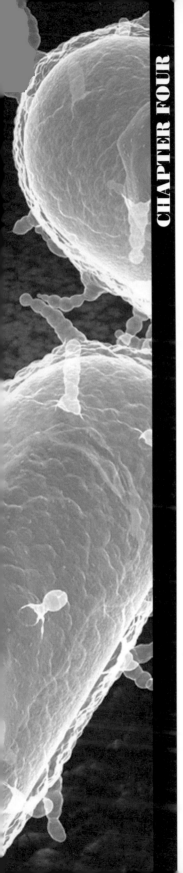

CHAPTER FOUR

REBUILDING SOCIETY

Europe crumbled under the attacks of the plague. Crops were left to rot in the fields. Livestock roamed free—or died from neglect or disease. (The plague killed many animals, too.) The barns were open; the houses were left empty. Normal sights and sounds of life had been replaced with disorganization and an eerie quiet.

A Silver Lining

In the face of so much death, it's difficult to think that anything good might have come from the plague. Historians agree it dramatically changed life in Europe. However, some of this change actually helped the people who survived.

In the three hundred years leading up to the outbreak in 1347, Europe's population had grown considerably. The continent was beginning to show some strain. Cities became more crowded. The standard of living declined for people who were not wealthy. By the time the plague hit, many Europeans were slipping toward subsistence living. In other words, they were producing barely enough food to survive. Famines were starting to occur. Hunger was a

In addition to disease, famine killed many people in Europe's cities, villages, and countryside. After the enormous loss of population, survivors had to find new ways of fitting into society.

daily misery for many. Disaster was just around the corner: all it would take was some natural catastrophe that would interrupt the ability to grow food. The disaster that came, of course, was the plague. In fact, during the plague, many people died of starvation as well as disease. However, this mass death did one good thing: it left more resources for those who survived.

The survivors perhaps did not recognize this "silver lining." Their families, friends, and neighbors had died. Their businesses and towns were destroyed. However, these drastic changes set the stage for a new way of life. People fit into society in different ways.

The Decline of Feudalism

Medieval Europe was not a democracy. Instead, people were strictly divided into social classes. At the top was the nobility, led by a country's king. Under him were an assortment of barons, dukes, and knights. These men often owned large parcels

Peasants, or serfs, worked in the fields of their lords. Serfs were at the bottom of the social hierarchy before the plague. Afterward, they gained more economic power.

of land. They hired other people to manage the land, grow crops, and raise animals. Freemen—as their name implies—were free workers who were able to work for actual wages. At the bottom of this hierarchy were serfs, or peasants. Serfs were not paid in cash. They were bound to their lord (a member of the nobility) and were sworn to work his land. In return, they received the lord's protection and a small piece of land to use for themselves. This system was known as feudalism. (Clergy members, craftsmen, and merchants made up their own distinct classes.)

People were born into a certain class. It was not impossible to move to a different class, but it was not easy, either. The modern idea that hard work will lead to a better way of life is just that—a modern idea. For most medieval peasants, hard work only led to more hard work the next day. They were used to doing their jobs without complaining (at least not to their bosses).

The plague changed a lot of this. Suddenly, labor was scarce. Before the plague, owning land was desirable. Now, it was a huge responsibility. Land had to be tended, but there weren't enough people to tend it. Peasants began to realize that their services were valuable.

They had strong backs and capable hands. They knew how to grow food, care for animals, and make clothing—things that everyone needed.

After the plague, they approached their jobs with a whole new outlook. They demanded more money and better working conditions. Desperate landowners agreed. In some cases, serfs were paid in cash for the first time ever.

The tables had been turned. In England, landowners did not like the new system. They had less power. Their fortunes were slipping away. They complained to their king, Edward III. As a noble, it was not surprising that he sided with the landowners. He passed laws that set wages back at their pre-plague levels. These laws were not always obeyed. Laborers still demanded more money. Landowners still paid it. Both

How Do I Look?

Silk veils, sable fur, and silver buckles: these were the designer outfits of medieval Europe. After the first wave of the plague, some people had more money than ever before. They bought fancy furs and colorful clothing—items that only rich people could afford previously. Fashions became more daring. Coats got shorter and dresses got tighter.

The nobility was worried that peasants were forgetting their place. In 1363, England's King Edward III passed a new set of sumptuary laws. Among other things, these laws dictated what people could wear. Fabrics and colors were regulated. The sizes of sleeves and the lengths of trains were all clearly spelled out. The higher up in the social order someone was, the better the clothes he or she was allowed to wear. However, law or no law, many people wore whatever they wanted to.

sides could be fined if they broke these laws, but the reality of getting work done sometimes mattered more than the law.

Rules were also passed to remind peasants of their social status. There was to be no swearing and no playing dice, for example. Later, the English government passed several poll taxes, which were sort of like income taxes. Many people thought these taxes were unfair. Finally, the peasants had had enough. In 1381, they revolted.

The revolt itself failed. There were a few bloody incidents, but King Richard II (who was only fourteen) was able to regain control. He agreed to change things. Afterward, however, the king's advisers did not follow through on these promises. The leaders of the rebellion were hanged. However, the revolt was a key event in the decline of feudalism.

Similar rebellions happened in France and Italy. They did not always change things. But they showed that peasants were ready to stand up for their rights.

Advances in Technology

There is a saying: necessity is the mother of invention. This means that people find new ways of doing things because they have to. In the decades following the plague, there was a huge need for work.

In the past, the vast majority of work had been done by human workers. With fewer workers, people started finding other ways—mechanical ways—to get things done.

Life continued. There was land to be farmed. Goods needed to be sold, traded, and shipped. Wars had to be fought. With fewer bodies to do these things, people came up with more efficient ways to accomplish their goals.

In sea travel, for example, ships got bigger and crews got smaller. That meant they could carry more goods, while also cutting labor costs. To pull this off, the quality of ship construction improved. Navigational instruments got better. These changes helped the craftsmen who built the ships, as well as the sailors who manned them.

Workers with tools are shown in this fifteenth-century illustration, which appeared in a translation of a book about famous men written by Giovanni Boccaccio. The Italian author lived during the plague.

Fewer soldiers to fight wars led to the invention of better weapons. Guns, it turned out, were more effective killers than spears or swords.

New ways of farming started. Some landowners converted farmland into pastureland. Raising animals required fewer workers than raising crops. Throughout England, for example, instead of growing wheat or barley, landowners started raising sheep. Because of this, wool and cloth grew into larger industries that would become a vital part of the country's economy.

Effects Outside Europe

Countries outside of Europe also had devastating losses from the plague, but the responses of people were not always the same.

For example, Christians questioned God's actions and became distraught at his lack of mercy. Muslims, on the other hand, quietly accepted the disease. While Europeans explored measures to stop the plague, such as quarantines, Muslims saw these as defying God's will. Muslim people also did not blame Jews or foreigners for the disease, as Europeans tended to do.

Timur was an Asian emperor who rose to power while the Black Death was sweeping Europe. He died in 1405, probably of plague, during a military campaign.

The plague wiped out rural populations and shriveled the economies of Muslim countries. Unlike in Europe however, there were no big leaps forward in technology or big changes in how resources were used. The European economy recovered by the fifteenth century. In other places it remained

stagnant. Like Europe, Egypt also lost about a third of its population. However, it did not experience the same political upheaval as was seen in parts of Europe.

It's also reasonable to expect that people who lived in China and on the steppes of Asia suffered huge losses from the plague. However, there are few written records to tell exactly what happened. The Mongol tribes who controlled the steppes were losing power by the middle of the fourteenth century. This may have been because plague was slaying them. The Mongols had come into power because they were formidable fighters and shrewd traders. Ironically, these skills may have actually helped to spread plague among them and to lead to their downfall.

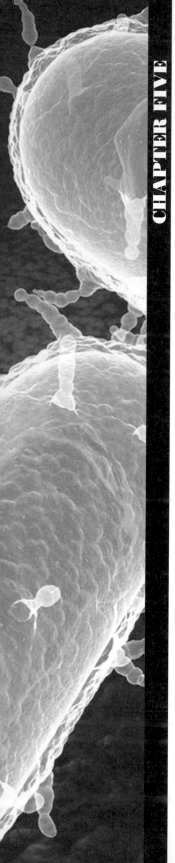

CHAPTER FIVE

PRELUDE TO THE RENAISSANCE

From the late 1300s into the 1600s, Europe experienced huge cultural changes. Previously, people had focused on the business of survival. Now, they looked to other interests. Art, literature, and education became more important. This explosion of culture was called the Renaissance.

The Renaissance affected Europe for centuries. A cultural movement that big cannot be pinned on a single event, not even one as big as the plague. However, historians believe the plague led to new attitudes that helped fuel the Renaissance.

A Crisis of Faith

As the plague raged through Europe, desperate people turned to the Catholic Church for help. However, with millions dying, it became more and more clear that priests and other clergy members had no power over the plague. They could not stop it in others, or even themselves.

Confused and shaken, people began to question the power of the clergy to serve as their ambassadors to God. Some people lost their faith

Martin Luther spoke out against the Catholic religion in the sixteenth century and became known as a Protestant. He and his followers are still remembered today in the Lutheran denomination of Christianity.

in God. Before the plague, the authority of the church was supreme. Afterward, it was not.

Some people began to treat religion differently. Instead of following the Catholic Church's rules exactly, they found approaches that worked for them as individuals. Formal religion lost a little of its grip.

The plague helped set the stage for a man named Martin Luther. In the early 1500s, Luther began speaking out against the church and some of its teachings. He even suggested that plague was evidence of God's displeasure with the Catholic Church. Because Luther protested the dominant religion, he became known as a Protestant. His opinions struck a chord with other Christians, as well. They believed in the basic teachings of Christ but did not always agree with how the Catholic Church interpreted those lessons. Christians became divided into Catholics and Protestants—the two major groups that still remain today.

Personal Lives

Plague made some people more pious. Others went the other way: they began to live more freely. They played more and worked less. Many people thought they would eventually die from plague, so they might as well enjoy themselves while they could. However, there was a sense of desperation as well. Agnolo di Tura, in his plague account, observed survivors in Siena, Italy. "Everyone appeared to be rich because they had

Women sell fruits and vegetables at a market stall in this fresco from the fifteenth century. As Europe entered the Renaissance, people had more economic opportunities.

survived and regained value in life," he wrote. "Now, no one knows how to put their life back in order."

The nature of marriage also changed, but again, not always in the same way. In some areas, there were fewer marriages. Perhaps the grim effect of the plague killed the desire to celebrate. Also, people did not know what the future held. Life had become extremely fragile. In some cases people simply lived for themselves. They did not think much about the next generation.

In other places the reverse happened. Instead of waiting until they were more secure in their lives, people got married even younger. They wanted to start their families and begin rebuilding the population.

The plague affected other family functions, too, such as inheritance. When a man died, his money and property typically went to his oldest son. After the plague, many of the oldest sons were dead, too. Now, younger sons—and sometimes even daughters—got to use this money to establish themselves.

The changing economy affected people's personal and professional lives profoundly. Many found themselves with more money than they had ever had. Some artistic professions had lost many of their members to the plague. This created vacancies that young workers were eager to fill. Women were offered more opportunities as well. The strict divisions of class and gender began to blur. Every set of hands was needed, no matter who they belonged to.

Art, Literature, and Education

Art and architecture underwent dramatic changes. Part of this was because of the changed structure of guilds. People who specialized in certain professions, such as carpentry, masonry

Story Time

Giovanni Boccaccio was a writer who lived in Florence, Italy, during the plague.

While the disease was ravaging the city, Boccaccio wrote *The Decameron*. The characters in the book flee the city trying to escape the plague. They then tell each other stories to entertain themselves. The book has one hundred different stories!

Scholars think the work is important because it shows how people dealt with the terror of the plague. In the book, the characters are trying to create an island of happiness for themselves amid all the death.

The book was popular at the time and is still considered Boccaccio's masterpiece. However, later in his life, Boccaccio criticized his own work. He called it "less than decent." He wrote in a letter to a friend, "I am certainly not pleased that you have allowed the illustrious women in your house to read my trifles; indeed, I beg you to give me your word that you will not permit it." Who knows what Boccacio would say if he found out his book had been translated into numerous languages and even made into movies.

(bricklaying), painting, or embroidery, were called craftsmen. Craftsmen belonged to associations called guilds. Traditionally, people who wanted to enter into these professions started as apprentices. They learned from someone who already knew what to do. An apprentice could work for several years learning his trade. He was not paid but received food and a place to live.

After the plague, there were fewer people available. Apprenticeships began at a younger age and might not last as long. There was a downside, as well. The plague had killed off a lot of the experts. Certain skills died out along with the people who had mastered them. For example, England had a

Men in Venice's sawmill workers' guild are shown in this eighteenth-century panel. The rules and operations of many guilds changed dramatically after the plague, to accommodate fewer workers.

group of craftsmen who made exquisite miniatures. So many of them died that the art form itself suffered.

Perhaps the influence of the plague was most obvious in painting. After the plague, death was a popular theme in art.

Artists often included an element called "the Dance of Death." In this, a figure that represented Death (often a skeleton) led a parade of people to their graves. Another trend in art was painting portraits. People were more concerned with their individual interests and accomplishments. Also, they wanted to be remembered. A natural way to express this was by having one's portrait painted.

Several universities dotted Europe at the time the plague hit. Some of these, battered by death, simply ceased to exist. New ones sprang up afterward. Most universities had used Latin as their main language. England's grammar schools used French. However, there weren't enough people left who knew how to speak Latin. No one had time to teach children French. After the plague there was a switch to the common language—English.

The Plague Returns

"The Black Death" refers to a period of about four years, from 1347 to 1351. This period, though intense, was only one outbreak of plague in Europe during the second pandemic.

More outbreaks occurred throughout the rest of the fourteenth century. Only ten years after the Black Death, in 1361, another epidemic hit. This one was sometimes called the children's plague. It killed many young people. This might have

This engraving shows what Windsor Castle looked like during the sixteenth-century reign of Queen Elizabeth I. She escaped London and fled to the castle during outbreaks of the plague.

been because older people had acquired some immunity from the plague a decade earlier. More outbreaks occurred throughout the fifteenth and sixteenth centuries.

Queen Elizabeth I was terrified of plague. When it came to London in 1563, the queen fled to Windsor Castle (about twenty-three miles [thirty-seven kilometers] away). She had a gallows built and ordered that anyone trying to enter Windsor from London be hanged.

Fifteen years later, the plague appeared again. This time, Elizabeth outlawed many public gatherings. Restaurants and pubs closed their doors. The queen even issued a royal order for doctors to find a cure. In 1593 and 1594, London's theaters—including Shakespeare's famous Globe Theatre—were closed in a desperate attempt to stop the plague. During times of plague, cities often passed stricter sanitation laws. However, these laws tended to relax when there was no threatening epidemic. Even into the nineteenth century, European cities were filthy places that led to the spread of disease.

These later outbreaks were shorter and killed far fewer people. However, in 1665, a major epidemic hit London. This was called the Great Plague. It killed about 15 percent of London's population. A huge fire the next year demolished a large part of the city. The fire also killed many rats, which may have helped stop the plague.

The Scientific Method

Doctors had failed miserably in their efforts to fight the plague. Afterward, the whole medical profession was questioned.

In the medieval period, medicine was still practiced according to the teachings of Galen. Galen was a physician who had lived in the second century. He was a brilliant thinker for his time. He did important research that helped physicians understand the circulatory and nervous systems.

By the time of the Black Death, more than one thousand years had passed since Galen's time. Little research or progress had been made in medicine. Doctors were still using information that was centuries old. Not surprisingly, a lot of it was wrong. It hurt doctors' efforts to fight the disease.

After the plague, physicians began to collect more information. The church did not allow autopsies (dissecting a corpse in order to learn about the body and its processes). However, in the centuries to follow, medicine put new emphasis on anatomy. If illness were ever to be cured, doctors had to understand how the body worked. The discovery of what caused the plague was still centuries in the future. But people were beginning to ask questions. After the plague, no one took anything for granted—even traditions were questioned.

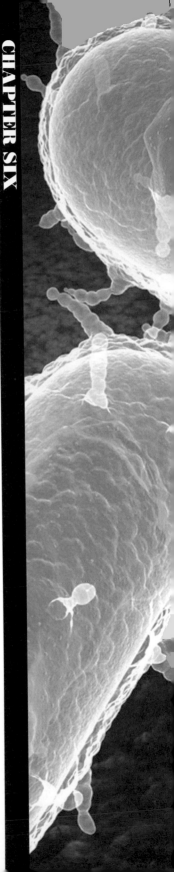

CHAPTER SIX

A MODERN THREAT?

Plague never goes away. It is always around, waiting for the right circumstances for an attack. When the third pandemic occurred in the nineteenth century, nobody was ready for it. However, scientists were better equipped to study it.

Fighting Back

The plague raged in the Far East in the 1890s. Alexandre Yersin, a scientist from France, traveled to Hong Kong. A plague hospital had been established there, but Yersin was not allowed in. Instead, he had to work out of a small hut next door. It was there that Yersin identified the bacteria that caused the plague. He also showed that the same bacteria inhabited both humans and rats. However, Yersin still did not know how the disease passed from rats to people.

That discovery came from Paul-Louis Simond, another French scientist. He observed that people who came into contact with dead or sick rats also came down with the plague. He also noticed that the sick rats had a lot of fleas. Could fleas be carrying the disease? Simond put

Despite difficult working conditions, French scientist Alexandre Yersin identified the plague bacteria in 1894 during an outbreak in Hong Kong. He also showed that rats carried the disease.

two rats—one sick and one healthy—in separate wire cages and placed them close together. The rats could not touch each other—but their fleas could easily jump back and forth. Sure enough, the healthy rat got sick.

Scientists now knew what the plague bacteria looked like. They knew how the disease was transmitted. The next step was to develop a vaccine. Many vaccines work by infecting a person with a small dose of disease bacteria. The body then develops antibodies that can fight them. If the person is later exposed to the disease, his or her body will already have the weapons needed to resist. In 1896, a man named Waldemar Haffkine created a vaccine using dead plague bacteria. Thousands of people were vaccinated against the plague. Interestingly, Haffkine was Jewish. Jews had been erroneously blamed for the Black Death, but a Jewish person saved people from the plague.

Plague could be avoided and even prevented. But it still could not be cured. That step finally occurred in the 1940s with the development of antibiotics that killed bacteria living in a person's body.

Plague in California

One of the scariest aspects of the third pandemic of plague was how it traveled. It was not confined to one area. Instead, it jumped all over the world. In 1900, plague reached the United States by way of San Francisco.

The first death was in March of 1900. A struggle between San Francisco's leaders followed. Health officials wanted to take measures to stop the spread of plague. Other politicians pretended the disease was a minor problem if it existed at all.

In 1900, the United States' first case of plague was reported in San Francisco, California. People in the city's Chinatown area were believed to be spreading the disease.

After a worker in San Francisco's Chinatown died of the plague, the state board of health quarantined the area. Chinese residents protested the quarantine. They said it was discrimination. California's governor, Henry Gage, also fought the idea of the plague. He didn't want it to damage California's reputation. He dismissed doctors' reports and tried to keep the federal government from getting involved. The resistance to admit what was happening gave the plague enough time to spread. The death toll was minor, however, compared with previous outbreaks. Probably less than three hundred people died by the end of the outbreak in 1908.

In 1924, a Latino man in East Los Angeles found a dead rat under his house. Within days, both he and his teenage daughter were sick with bubonic plague. Both died. Records show that authorities probably knew that plague had caused the deaths. However, they did not admit to an outbreak of the disease. In the next few days, several more people died. Still, it took more than three weeks for a doctor to set up a special hospital ward for the plague patients. It took even longer to quarantine the area where the outbreak started. By the time it ended, about thirty-seven people had died. Once again, the stigma attached to the disease had kept authorities quiet.

San Francisco's Most Wanted

When the plague hit San Francisco in 1900, officials decided to fight the disease by going for the rats. A doctor named Rupert Blue was in charge. He knew rats were picky eaters, so he whipped up an appetizing bait of cheese, bacon, apples, and carrots. He hired workers to trap the rats, but they couldn't catch enough. Blue decided to let anyone trap rats. He would pay 10 cents per rat.

After the 1906 earthquake, plague broke out again in San Francisco. Blue brought back his rat-catching program. He and his team wrote up detailed instructions on how to catch rats. And the price had gone up: 25 cents for a male, and 50 cents for a breeding female. By the time the rat campaign ended, it's estimated that more than two million rats were killed. That's five rats for every person who lived in the city.

India in 1994

In 1993, a major earthquake rocked India. Scientists believe it drove wild rats—who carried plague—out of their homes. They spread the disease to rats that lived in the city of Surat. These rats then passed the plague to people.

The first human case came in 1994. The government was caught by surprise. Rumors and hysteria spread much faster than the disease itself. People panicked. First, they jammed into pharmacies to buy antibiotics. Then, they left the city. Within days, about three hundred thousand people had fled. Other cities in India were afraid all these people might bring the plague with them. Finally, the police stepped in to stop people from leaving.

With masks over their faces to keep out the germs, people jammed the streets of Surat, India, in 1994, trying to flee the city during a plague outbreak.

The plague in Surat was pneumonic, and it was very contagious. The city shut down. Officials closed schools, movie theaters, and public spaces. When people had to leave their homes, they walked the streets with their faces covered. Despite the initial panic, the government was able to regain

control and establish safety measures. Only about fifty people died in the epidemic.

However, there were huge financial effects. The city was gearing up for a large annual festival. Instead, thousands of tourists canceled their plans to visit. Other countries temporarily refused to import products made in India. This cost the nation's economy millions of dollars.

Future dangers

Modern science can identify the plague. Modern medicine can treat it if a person gets infected. What modern technology cannot do is get rid of it. In many parts of the world, plague is endemic. This means it exists at a low level, only passing between animals. But sometimes it erupts and spreads to humans.

Plague is endemic to several places around the world. One of these is the southwestern United States. It is mostly found in prairie dogs and squirrels in Arizona and New Mexico, as well as parts of California, Nevada, Utah, Colorado, and Oregon. According to the Centers for Disease Control and Prevention, about ten to twenty people get the plague each year in the United States. About 14 percent of those die.

Prairie dogs, along with rats, squirrels, and other rodents, can carry the plague bacteria. The disease is regularly found in animal populations in the southwestern United States.

Worldwide, anywhere from one thousand to three thousand cases of plague occur each year.

Like most diseases, plague is always changing. In 1995, a patient was diagnosed with a strain of plague that regular antibiotics could not kill. In this case, doctors found different

Punishment by Plague

In the 1930s and 1940s, Japan was at war with China. A Japanese army general, Shiro Ishii, was determined to kill his enemies any way he could. Ishii ordered dozens of medical "experiments" to discover how to do this. These actions were, in fact, some of the worst forms of torture.

One of his horrific ideas was to infect his enemies with diseases, including plague. Plague-infested fleas were loaded into huge bombs and dumped over China. They killed thousands—perhaps hundreds of thousands—of people. Then the wind started blowing the other direction. Now the fleas were moving toward Japan. Japanese soldiers were killed as well. Only then did Ishii call off the bombings.

drugs to do the job. However, it was a scary preview of what could happen. If available antibiotics were unable to kill the plague bacteria, it could mean severe trouble if there were a large outbreak.

Few words are as scary to humans as the word "plague." Even though plague is rare today, it still occurs. And even though medicine usually helps, it doesn't always. More than once, it has brought civilization to its knees, killing millions and drastically changing the lives of the survivors. Yet many of those changes helped shape the world we live in today. In a strange way, we owe our lives to the plague.

TEN GREAT QUESTIONS
to ask a DOCTOR

1 What can I do to avoid ever catching the plague?

2 What types of antibiotics are used to treat the plague?

3 Where can I go to learn more about the history of the plague?

4 Can you catch the plague from a pet rat?

5 What are the chances of a new outbreak of the plague?

6 Should I be worried about the plague if my dog has fleas?

7 How is the plague transmitted?

8 How many cases of the plague occur in a year?

9 How is pneumonic plague different from bubonic plague?

10 How is the plague diagnosed?

GLOSSARY

antibiotic A substance or compound that kills or inhibits the reproduction of bacteria.

antibody A protein made by the body's immune system to fight off infections.

bioterrorism Terrorism by intentional release or dissemination of bacteria, viruses, or toxins.

bubo A swelling of the lymph nodes, appearing under the armpit, in the groin, or on the neck.

bubonic Referring to an infection that enters through the skin and travels through the lymphatics.

endemic Describes an infection that is contained within a particular population.

epidemic The occurrence of a disease beyond what is normal.

exquisite Exceptionally beautiful and well formed.

grisly Gruesome; horrible.

hysteria Intense agitation or panic.

infested Inhabited by a large number of pests.

lymph node An organ that acts as a filter or trap for foreign particles.

outbreak An occurrence of a disease greater than would be expected in a particular time and place.

pandemic The occurrence of a disease that spreads across an entire region or worldwide; it is larger than an epidemic.

pestilence A powerful, infectious disease; this originally referred to bubonic plague.

pious Very religious; devout.

pneumonic Referring to an infection that enters through the air passages and infects the lungs.

quarantine The practice of isolating sick people from healthy people.

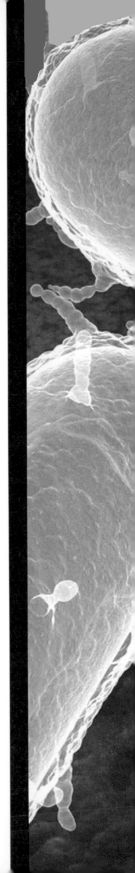

ravage To cause destruction and pain.

repent To show regret for past actions and willingness to make amends.

scapegoat Someone who is wrongly blamed.

septicemic Referring to an infection that occurs when bacteria enter the blood from the lymphatic and respiratory systems.

stagnant Still; unchanging.

subsistence Existing at a minimum level.

sumptuary Relating to the use of luxury items.

vulnerable More likely to be hurt.

FOR MORE INFORMATION

Centers for Disease Control and Prevention
1600 Clifton Road
Atlanta, GA 30333
(800) 232-4636
Web site: http://www.cdc.gov
The CDC collects and maintains information on diseases affecting people worldwide as well as providing resources to combat disease.

Center for the History of Global Health and Disease
History of Medicine
Johns Hopkins University
School of Medicine
Welch Library, 3rd Floor
1900 East Monument Street
Baltimore, MD 21205-2113
Web site: http://www.hopkinsmedicine.org/histmed/
programs/history_disease
Programs at this center focus on studying the history of diseases from both medical and social perspectives.

Centre for Medieval Studies
University of Toronto
125 Queen's Park, 3rd Floor
Toronto, ON M5S 2C7
Canada
(416) 978-4884
Web site: http://www.chass.utoronto.ca/medieval
The Centre for Medieval Studies coordinates university programs about medieval history and culture.

Medieval Academy of America
104 Mount Auburn Street, 5th Floor

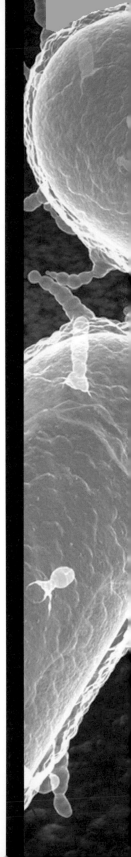

Cambridge, MA 02138
(617) 491-1622
Web site: http://www.medievalacademy.org
This professional organization is devoted to research and education in the field of medieval studies.

National Foundation for Infectious Diseases
4733 Bethesda Avenue
Suite 750
Bethesda, MD 20814
(301) 656-0003
Web site: http://www.nfid.org
The NFID is a nonprofit organization devoted to educating the public and health professionals about infectious diseases.

National Library of Medicine
8600 Rockville Pike
Bethesda, MD 20894
(888) 346-3656
Web site: http://www.nlm.nih.gov
Part of the National Institutes of Health, the library helps promote biomedical research and public health by providing information to both the public and medical professionals.

Public Health Agency of Canada
130 Colonnade Road
A.L. 6501H
Ottawa, ON K1A 0K9
Canada
Web site: http://www.phac-aspc.gc.ca
The PHAC works to improve the overall health of Canadians as well as control diseases and respond to health emergencies.

World Health Organization
Avenue Appia 20
1211 Geneva 27
Switzerland
Web site: http://www.who.int
Operated through the United Nations, the WHO sets policies
and directs research efforts on global health issues.

Web Sites

Due to the changing nature of Internet links, Rosen Publishing
has developed an online list of Web sites related to the subject
of this book. This site is updated regularly. Please use this
link to access the list:

http://www.rosenlinks.com/epi/plag

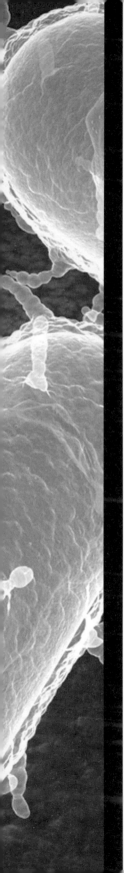

FOR FURTHER READING

Anderson, Dale. *Churches and Religion in the Middle Ages.* Strongsville, OH: Gareth Stevens Publishing, 2005.

Barnard, Bryn. *Outbreak! Plagues that Changed History.* New York, NY: Crown Books for Young Readers, 2005.

Brooks, Geraldine. *Year of Wonders.* New York, NY: Penguin, 2002.

Corrick, James A. *The Early Middle Ages.* San Diego, CA: Lucent Books, 2005.

Corrick, James A. *The Renaissance.* San Diego, CA: Lucent Books, 2006.

Dahme, Joanne. *The Plague.* Philadelphia, PA: Running Press Kids, 2009.

Dawson, Ian. *Medicine in the Middle Ages.* Brooklyn, NY: Enchanted Lion Books, 2005.

Emmeluth, Donald. *Plague.* New York, NY: Chelsea House, 2005.

Farrell, Janette. *Invisible Enemies.* New York, NY: Farrar, Straus and Giroux, 2005.

Friedlander, Mark P., Jr. *Outbreak: Disease Detectives at Work.* Minneapolis, MN: Twenty-First Century Books, 2009.

Goldsmith, Connie. *Invisible Invaders: Dangerous Infectious Diseases.* Minneapolis, MN: Twenty-First Century Books, 2006.

Herbst, Judith. *Germ Theory.* Minneapolis, MN: Twenty-First Century Books, 2007.

Levitin, Sonia. *The Cure.* New York, NY: Silver Whistle (Harcourt Brace & Company), 1999.

Oldfield, Pamela. *The Great Plague: A London Girl's Diary, 1665–1666.* New York, NY: Scholastic, 2008.

Rose, Simon. *The Heretic's Tomb.* Vancouver, BC: Tradewind Books, 2008.

Senker, Cath. *The Black Death 1347–1350: The Plague Spreads Across Europe.* Chicago, IL: Raintree, 2006.

Snedden, Robert. *The Medieval World.* Philadelphia, PA: Saunders Book Co., 2009.

Townsend, John. *Pox, Pus, and Plague: A History of Disease and Infection.* Chicago, IL: Raintree Publishers, 2005.

Walker, Richard. *Epidemics and Plagues.* Boston, MA: Kingfisher Publications, 2006.

Zahler, Diane. *The Black Death.* Minneapolis, MN: Twenty-First Century Books, 2009.

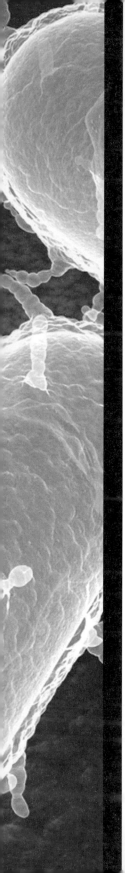

BIBLIOGRAPHY

Aberth, John. *The Black Death*. Boston, MA: Bedford/ St. Martin's, 2005.

Baillie, Mike. *New Light on the Black Death*. Stroud, Gloucestershire, England: Tempus Publishing Limited, 2006.

Benedictow, Ole J. *The Black Death*. Woodbridge, Suffolk, England: The Boydell Press, 2004.

Cantor, Norman F. *In the Wake of the Plague*. New York, NY: Free Press, 2001.

Centers for Disease Control. "The History of Bioterrorism: Plague." CDC.gov. Retrieved May 30, 2009 (http://www.bt.cdc.gov/training/ historyofbt/03plague.asp).

Centers for Disease Control. "Plague Information." CDC.gov. Retrieved May 17, 2009 (http://www. bt.cdc.gov/agent/plague/index.asp).

Chase, Marilyn. *The Barbary Plague*. New York, NY: Random House, 2003.

Feldinger, Frank. *A Slight Epidemic*. Aberdeen, WA: Silver Lake Publishing, 2008.

Gottfried, Robert S. *The Black Death*. New York, NY: The Free Press, 1983.

Herlihy, David, with Samuel K. Cohn, Jr., ed. *The Black Death and the Transformation of the West*. Cambridge, MA: Harvard University Press, 1997.

Ibeji, Mike. "Black Death: Political and Social Changes." BBC.co.uk. Retrieved May 12, 2009 (http://www.bbc.co.uk/history/british/middle_ages/ blacksocial_01.shtml).

Kelly, John. *The Great Mortality*. New York, NY: HarperCollins, 2005.

McNeill, William H. *Plagues and Peoples*. Garden City, NY: Anchor Press, 1976.

New York University. "Black Death: Catastrophic Disease in Human History." NYU.edu. Retrieved May 12, 2009 (http://www.nyu.edu/projects/mediamosaic/bd.html).

Nohl, Johannes, ed. *The Black Death: A Chronicle of the Plague.* London, England: George Allen & Unwin, Ltd., 1926.

Orent, Wendy. *Plague.* New York, NY: Free Press, 2004.

Smith, Christine A. "Plague in the Ancient World: A Study from Thucydides to Justinian." *The Student Historical Journal, 1996–1997.* Loyno.edu. Retrieved May 15, 2009 (http://www.loyno.edu/~history/journal/1996-7/Smith.html).

Stefani, Marchione Di Coppo. *The Florentine Chronicle.* Retrieved May 29, 2009 (http://www2.iath.virginia.edu/osheim/marchione.html).

World Resources Institute. "The Black Death Revisited: India's 1994 Plague Epidemic." WRI.org. Retrieved May 29, 2009 (http://archive.wri.org/page.cfm?id=941&page=pubs_content_text).

Ziegler, Philip. *The Black Death.* New York, NY: Harper & Row, 1969.

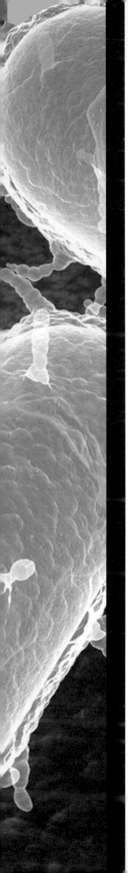

INDEX

About the Author

Diane Bailey has always been interested in gruesome diseases, with their frightening symptoms and often fatal outcomes. While researching this book and another in the series, *Cholera*, she was fascinated to learn how diseases have changed entire societies. Diane lives in Kansas and writes on a variety of nonfiction topics for teens.

Photo Credits

Cover (left), back cover (right) © www.istockphoto.com/adisa; cover (right), back cover (left) pp. 7, 16, 26, 38, 48, 59, 69, 71, 74, 76, 78 Shutterstock.com; pp. 4–5 Private Collection/The Bridgeman Art Library; pp. 8–9, 11 CDC; pp. 14–15, 27, 62 Courtesy of the National Library of Medicine; p. 17 San Vitale, Ravenna, Italy/Giraudon/The Bridgeman Art Library; pp. 20–21 Art Museum of Yaroslavl, Russia/The Bridgeman Art Library; p. 23 Private Collection/Archives Charmet/The Bridgeman Art Library; p. 29 National University Library, Prague, Czech Republic/The Bridgeman Art Library (detail of illustrated page); p. 31 Bibliotheque Nationale, Paris, France/The Bridgeman Art Library/Getty Images; pp. 32–33 British Library, London, Great Britain/HIP/Art Resource, NY; p. 35 Private Collection/The Bridgeman Art Library; pp. 39, 44–45 British Library, London, UK © British Library Board. All Rights Reserved/The Bridgeman Art Library; pp. 40–41 Private Collection/The Bridgeman Art Library/Getty Images; pp. 46–47 Louvre, Paris, France/The Bridgeman Art Library/Getty Images; p. 49 Stock Montage/Hulton Archive/Getty Images; pp. 50–51 Castello di Issogne, Val d'Aosta, Italy/Giraudon/The Bridgeman Art Library/Getty Images; pp. 54–55 Museo Correr, Venice, Italy/The Bridgeman Art Library; pp. 56–57 Hulton Archive/Getty Images; p. 60 Archives Larousse, Paris, France/Giraudon/The Bridgeman Art Library; pp. 64–65 Raveendran/AFP/Getty Images; p. 66 Justin Sullivan/Getty Images.

Designer: Sam Zavieh; Editor: Bethany Bryan;
Photo Researcher: Peter Tomlinson